Lord, I'm Dancin' As Fast As I Can

Lord, I'm Dancin' As Fast as I Can

Selected Poems

J. Joy Matthews Alford

Introduction by Dorothy Gilliam

Thelemaque Publishing
A Division of Thelemaque Associates L.L.C

Published in the United States by
Thelemaque Publishing

ISBN: 0-972-443495 paper

LCCN 2003100222

For my children

Ronald, Joy and Brian,

and in Memory of my parents

Marjorie and John

Acknowledgments

I first thank God for the Gift of His Word. He has blessed me with several faithful friends and loved ones, through whose encouragement, patience and persistence (that I continue my journey) this collection of poems has come to life.

Thank you to my sisters, Brenda, Marjorie, Bessie, Annette and Shirley; and my brothers Ray and George for the "growin' up" years of love and the late midnight hours of listening to poetry over the phone.

Thank you to Rev. Benjamin and Lillie Craig for the testimony of God's mercy and love. Thank you to Frances (Yvonne) Hicks and Frank Peace for unwavering friendship, and teaching me to summon up my own "sterner stuff" when my valleys get low.

Thank you with special blessings of love and gratitude to Billye Okera, Sylvia Dianne Beverly-Patterson, Carolyn Joyner, Angela Boykin, and my sister-in-the-word who now sojourns a higher road; Margie Jones, for the special love and spiritual blessing of sisterhood through Collective Voices.

Thank you to my "music family" that faithfully supports and accompanies me during readings and performances, in particular, Doc Powell, Sydney March, Donna Curtis and Vince Evans.

Thank you to long-time friends and supporters Valerie Kyer, Regina Bromery, John Pressley, Alan Gregory, Skip Kelly, Terri Allen, Ginger Clark, Sandra Jowers, Ethelbert Miller, Eleanor Dore, Chuck Hicks, Acie Byrd, David Chaytor, Brother

Ah and The Jazz Collectors, Jan Summers, Rev. Dr. Grainger Browning, Jr., Rev. Dr. Jo Ann Browning, Sis. Lottie Sneed, Patricia Alford (and all the family), Nettie Bloodsaw, Joyce Flowers, Karen and Caleb Gray-Burris, Kenneth Walker, Ann Moore, Dori Sanders and Jane Graf.

Thank you to my "It's Your Mug" family from whom I learned the value of group workshops, and that artistic integrity is the only standard by which poetry can be measured.

Special thanks to my long time friend and publisher of ACE-Dialogue Magazine, Benita Dale.

Thank you Dale and Terri Allen, publishers of this poetry collection for guidance and patience as I navigated the foreign waters of publishing contracts.

A very special thank-you to Dolores Kendrick, Poet Laureate of Washington, DC, for her support and for including me in the Poets In Progress reading series following which this book was initially released.

Lastly, I most graciously and humbly wish to thank Dorothy Gilliam award winning Washington Post journalist, to whom I am eternally indebted for embracing and introducing my first poetry book with words that reached inside and touched the core of the healing channel which, for me poetry has always been.

TABLE OF CONTENTS

Introduction 11

My Soul Shouts Out Loud 13

Strong Hands of Mother Africa 14
Lifeline 15
Balance of Power 17
Dreams, Nightmares and Storms 18
Malcolm's Legacy 19
A Child's Query 21
John Brown's Legacy 23
Victors, Not Victims 24
Conditioned To React 25
With Honors 27
Change Sisters 30
Death Row Scenario 31
No Complicity 33
Victory Song 35

Reality Has No Rehearsals 37

Regrets 38
The Race 39
Why Not 40
Memories 42
My Mother's Smile 43
Visitation Rites 44
You, Like Me 45
I Be Dancin' 46
They Don't Play 48
This Thing I Do 50
Poetry Man 51

TABLE OF CONTENTS (cont.)

The Real Deal 53
Snapshots of Train #29 54
Giving Thanks..55
750 Horses (Virgin Ride)....................................57

Fuchsia, Sunshine and Blues 59

Coming Into Focus...60
Lower Left Side 61
All I Ever Wanted 62
Mourning..65
Please 66
The Gull 67
Consumed 68
The Scent 70
My Fine Chocolate Brother 71
Point Of No Return 72
Pork Chops And Twinkies 73

Tomorrow's Promise 75

Ode To My Ten-year-old Child 76
Beauty Parlor Mess 77
Just Around The Corner.....................................79
To See A Tree Sneeze..80
Ten Thousand Angels Dancing..........................81
Brian's Favorite Breakfast 83
Danielle's Picture...84
Blessings of Sister-Love 86

TABLE OF CONTENTS (cont.)

Brevity, Beauty and Basho – (Haiku)................89

Midnight Melodies..91
Morning Song..92
Spring Morn...93
Sweet Sounds...94
Mountain View...95
Winter's Warning..96
Digital Clock...97
School Zones..98

Reachin' Up..99

Get Outta' My Way.......................................100
Walk With Me Lord.......................................103
Chalices..106
We Wander...107
No Constraints..108
Sister To Sister..109
Basics..110
Whistling Winds..112
Hunger...113

Introduction

I am pleased to introduce Joy Matthews Alford's first book of poetry, *Lord, I'm Dancin' ...as Fast as I Can.* Alford is the founder of Collective Voices, a group of women poets in Washington, D.C. who have performed their works in the National Capital area for several years. Though this book is Alford's initial collection, hers is a seasoned voice of considerable depth and power.

The book's depth lies in Alford's clear understanding of what it means to be rooted in Africa while grounded in her experiences as a black woman in America. In the first cycle, "My Soul Shouts Out Loud," her poems mourn and celebrate the black experience--from the homeland from which blacks were stolen, through their sojourn in the new land. The poems bring Alford's pain for the deep wounds of her black brothers and sisters into clear focus. Yet she stands proudly among those who see the survival of African Americans as evidence of their strength, not their weakness. Despite the evidence she presents that blacks often are still strangers in a strange land, she sees blacks as victors, not victims.

Happily, Alford's range also embraces humor and love. "Fuscia, Sunshine and Blues," the second cycle in this book, is dominated by love poems that shift from sensuality to ecstasy to loss. From "My Fine Chocolate Brother" to "Point of No Return," Alford shows a responsive and receptive heart.

She also turns her sights on the black family--the love that holds it together and the challenges that can rip it apart. A poem dedicated to her daughter, "10 Thousand Angels," was especially enchanting.

Shining through many of Alford's poems is her strong faith in God, one of the main themes of "Reachin' Up," the final cycle in this book. This belief gives her courage and an optimism that helps her conquer obstacles. These works assure us that black people will continue their fight for equality and she will heal her broken heart. With such an impressive beginning, we can only look forward to the future offerings of poet J. Joy Matthews Alford, a.k.a. "Sistah Joy."

Dorothy Gilliam
October 2000

My Soul Shouts Out Loud

STRONG HANDS OF MOTHER AFRICA

Strong hands of Mother Africa
Awaken places deep inside me
Where my ancestors dwell
Like distant echoes, your heart-beat
Reverberates off Kilimanjaro's mountain-tops
Pulses down the Nile
Crosses the Sudan
And flows into my soul

Strong hands of Mother Africa
Call my absent spirit
To return and commune with the elders
Those who sojourned before me
Now light my path
And await my homecoming

Strong hands of Mother Africa
Reveal to me my history
Teach me the ways of my true homeland
Unmask the mysteries and tragedies of this
altered consciousness
Awaken in my mind and body
The unripened seeds of truth, power, and pride

Solve for me the paradox of my mortality
Strong hands of Mother Africa
My soul dances to your ancient rhythm
Pulsing, ever pulsing, through the veins of time
Teach me to beat Africa drums
So that I, too, may guide
Another absent spirit to your shores
So that I, too, may guide another absent spirit
- home

LIFELINE

The sweet sultry sound of your sax
Melts me like wax.

Melodious rainbows painted
From the pulse of my people
Shower down through the sounds
Of midnight trombones.

Callused fingers caressing congas
Ricochet one off another
Beat strong, long into the night
As tales of woe and ecstasy
Spill through thick lips
Kissing a magic flute.

Syncopated beats from a thumpin' bass
Take us to a sacred place reserved just for us.
Where we dance to an ancient rhythm
Layin' claim to joy and pain all at the same
time.

All the while your mellifluous melodies
Awaken ancestral spirits within us.
We hear their silenced voices,
See visions of their dreams,
And rise to a new consciousness.

Many try to synthesize your sound
Try to imitate your orchestral symphony
With a Dixie-land band
But they can't understand your message

Can't comprehend the ebb of your flow
Anymore than they can understand
Ella's scats, Billie's blues, or Miles' Bitches Brew
For you are far more than sound
You are the lifeline of a people
Whose soul pulses through rhythm.
You are Jazz!

BALANCE OF POWER

We came to the table hungry
Carrying an empty plate
Despite your burgeoning plate
Threatening to collapse under its own weight
You were unwilling to share
Even so, you reached an outstretched hand
To take away our empty plate
When we withdrew
And insisted you had no right
You appeared stunned
We soon discovered that our plate
Was not empty after all
As we began to consume our portion
Your plate diminished
Again you reached out
This time with mallet in hand
Threatening to shatter our plate
It was then we recognized the look in your eye
We had never before looked you in the eye
For we had only sought
The bounty of your now empty plate
Amazed, we watched
As you recoiled in fear
As we watched
Our plate became laden
And overflowed.
Cautiously, ever so cautiously
We invited you to share
In our bounty

DREAMS, NIGHTMARES AND STORMS

Blind to the dreams of yesterday's visionaries
Today's victims of a tomorrow unrealized
Sit waiting
A King's dream has become relegated
To commemorative posters and archival tapes
Replayed time and time and time again
Against a backdrop of living nightmares
Sequels that cancel the extraordinary nature of both
What should have bound a people together
Lifted a people to heights of empowerment
Forged a people's course toward self-determination
Has withered
And sits in the corner
Listening to the sounds of silence
In the graveyards of our complacency
Waiting for the next storm to revive its roots

MALCOLM'S LEGACY

Life leaps by decades
When you're exposed to tragedy as a child
It marks you for eternity
Eradicating innocence
Obliterating boundaries
Shattering self-assuredness and esteem

Growth pains come hard
In a world that constrains a spirit
Determined to react in an equally profound
manner
Much weighs in the balance
Unfocused rage dictates retaliation
Until consciousness dictates creation
Of a pure heart
Of love for all human-kind
And, consequently, of self
Awakening the need to improve not just
one's own life
But the direction and quality of life throughout
one's world

Changing a world, even a universe
Becomes conceivable when, as a child
You've witnessed the destruction of your own

Malcolm changed a world
By stirring the souls and empowering the spirits
Of conditioned Negroes

Malcolm changed a world
By confronting the conscience of hypocrites
And challenging the presumptions and
practices of racists

Malcolm changed a world
By demanding accountability from political
and spiritual leaders

Malcolm changed a world
By learning to love, believe in, and cherish all
human life
Enabling the evolution of a people
To become the revolution of a Nationhood

Malcolm changed a world
Teaching that equality is borne
through integrity
And that for either to have meaning
Both must be maintained
Yes, by any means necessary

A CHILD'S QUERY

Will they free Mr. Mandela, Mama?
Will they finally set him free?
You said he's been jailed for twenty-seven years.
How much longer will it be?

Why was he put in jail, Mama?
What did he really do?
You said he helped his people.
Did he help me and you?

They freed Nelson Mandela, Mama!
I just saw him on TV.
You said he was a great fighter.
He looks like an old man to me.

What is a political prisoner, Mama?
Are all Black politicians sent to jail?
Is Mr. Mandela's government afraid of him?
Can he make their system fail?

What does "Apartheid" mean, Mama?
What kind of government is that?
Does it mean that in South Africa
Whites should be in control of Blacks?

Why should anyone be in charge, Mama
Just because of their race?
Isn't it what's in your heart and mind
that counts
Not the color of your face?

If South African Blacks can't vote, Mama
Nor own any property,
If they can't buy a house, or even a car,
What a sad place that must be.

I don't think Apartheid is right, Mama.
How did it ever start?
How could anyone think it would
help the world
To keep people apart?

I'm glad they freed Mr. Mandela, Mama.
I hope he lives to see
The kind of world he's fought for
Where all people live in harmony.

If Mr. Mandela came to America, Mama
What would he think of our democracy?
What would he think of our neighborhood?
What would he think of me?

JOHN BROWN'S LEGACY

Who would stand, fight, die for right
Often ridiculed, who would so choose
Martyrdom gives no glory
To which cynics are honor-bound
Hangman's noose swings freely
In more hearts now than ever swung
in Charlestown
And bullets quickly find folks who stand
their ground

Old causes finding new abolitionists
Take on lives of their own
Good chance they'll take more lives
than they have
Who will mourn their passing
Who will finally say "Enough!" and be heard
Who will remember the zealot
Who dared defy yesterday and today
Naively believing in tomorrow

VICTORS, NOT VICTIMS!

As you read documents of my slave-ship voyage
Or see depiction's of my bondage at sea
Know that my spirit reigned supreme
Both then and in the new land some claimed as free

Although my body bore shackles and chains
Understand that God's power sustains
Transforming even a slaver's chains
Into a mother's embrace
No longer chains, but pure love enfolding me
Yes, God's power sustains

I knew not where my path would lead
But, because today you know my story
Much to my enslaver's dismay
Even Malcolm, Marcus, and Moses
Rejoice as I claim my victory

The freedom my soul sought in darkest night
Shines today in your witness to my plight
For as long as you can remember and not relive
As long as you can shout out loud about the horror
And not fear the master's lash
As long as you can dance to the echo of my call
From graves at sea or branches of the magnolia tree
then I say, "Dance my sisters and brothers, dance!"
Dance to the rhythm of my voice
For I am with you still
And remember to list me
among the victors, not the victims
For I claim my victory in you

CONDITIONED TO REACT

Wake up young man
As you prepare for the war
Undisputedly targeting you
So focused on fighting to survive
Convinced you have neither the need nor time
To develop your mind
You believe money is the key to life
A key for which you're willing to pay any price
When the price is too high
It becomes the key to death

You never knew the price you'd pay
For gunshot blasts ringing
Through turbulent gangland mid-nights
Or peaceful playground mid-days
You thought revenge would repay your debt
For a brother's bloody corpse
Abandoned by you as the sirens grew too loud
But how could you have known
You have been conditioned to react

Conditioned not to think about living
Only surviving
Not about tomorrow
Only today
For you the war is already lost
It was lost when you bought your first gun
When you sold drugs to your neighbor's
Twelve-year-old son

When you decided the precious
gift of life was for sale
Just know that my son's life is not

You see, I too, have been conditioned to react
By gunshot blasts
That shatter the safety of my neighborhood
And drive-bys that miss their mark
But not the innocent child
Playing too near their bedroom window
By the reality that too many children
Can identify, and know how and where buy
Crack-cocaine and perceive such as a right of
passage into manhood
Yes, I too, have been conditioned to react
So to get to my son
You first have to get past me.

WITH HONORS

I graduated top of my class
Majored in Kick-Ass 101
From the School of Hard Knocks

Learned early not to cry the blues
'Cause if you can't cry 'em like Billie
Ain't nobody really listenin'

Learned to take what I need
Make what I need happen
Find my own sunshine and pray to my
own God

Learned that nothin' somebody else gives me
Is ever worth more than somethin' I earn
for myself
And I – I deserve everything good life
has to offer

So don't tell me what you're gonna do for me
How you're gonna take care of me
How you've got my back
Cause you see, I graduated
"Soon-I'll-Cum-Laud"

Soon I'll come Lord
To understand why empty houses stay boarded
While my sisters sleep on street grates at night

Soon I'll come Lord
To understand why farmers burn crops

While children starve around the world

Soon I'll come Lord
To understand why some choose to incarcerate
Rather than educate
Those who have been systematically excluded
From a society born largely of penal
colony expatriates

Soon I'll come Lord
To understand why governments
Can send people to the moon
Satellites into space
Can trace the dawn of distant stars
But can't intercept drugs
Crossing borders between neighboring
continents or cartels
Until then, I'll hand back your handouts
'Cause I see them as the put downs they
really are
And I'm turned off by your come-ons
'Cause coming or going
Your manipulations leave me – wanting

I reject your suggestion
That I should feel privileged
To live in a society
Where I am not respected
My man is the first suspected
And my children –
Lord, my children are the first to die

Yes, I graduated

Top of my class
And I've got my own back
'Cause based on my recollection of the past
I need to keep it just like that

CHANGE SISTERS

Change sisters change
Change ourselves inside out
Change to rise above somebody
else's game
Change to grow despite
Rugs pulled from under our feet
Knives twisted in our backs
Change to take back
What we should'a never
Gave away in the first place
Oh yes, sisters know how to change
You ain't seen change
Til you've seen a sister change
You see, our change comes with power
Power from another place
Power to change whenever we need
However we need
Change sisters
From burlap into brocade
Gabardine into gold
It's time sisters
To change into a true sisterhood

DEATH ROW SCENARIO

He walked to school that morning
Met his friends at the same bus stop
It was early in the day
So they didn't worry 'bout the cops

Weekday mornings it was safe
For them to be out on the street
But other times it was a crime
In the eyes of certain cops on the beat

His father used to tell him
How in his day they hung out at the park
But of course those days were long gone
He fit the profile after dark

Today was his 16th birthday
He'd celebrated after school with friends
But it got dark before they left
You know how this story ends

You see it was late November
It gets dark early that time of year
He stayed after school for his party
But he should've stashed his birthday gear

His friends had bought him lots of CDs
His backpack was loaded down
And when the cop stopped him for suspicion
One CD clattered to the ground

He tried to explain to the officer

"Not a gun" he tried to say
But the officer kept shouting "Don't move!"
Death row scenario was underway

In slow motion he saw the officer
Drop down on one bended knee
To retrieve the shiny object
That had fallen to the street

Just then his backpack started slipping
Off his shoulder and down his back
He tried to tell the cop why he'd moved
But it was much too late for that

His friends all ran for cover
They knew it was too late
His sixteenth birthday was his last
His profile had sealed his fate

NO COMPLICITY

My brother's pain rages forth
through the voice of my pen
With this mighty sword
I slay his villainous foe
for his enemy is mine
I cannot acknowledge his castration
and not be left barren
for his seed holds my promise of tomorrow
He has suffered generations of injustice
For it was his father
whose college degree
earned him a blue-collar job
but never the salary
of his blue-eyed college alumnus
It was his grandfather
who operated and opened elevator doors
in high-rise buildings
whose front doors were never open
to people like him
His great-grandfather
whose house was burnt to the ground
while he helped neighbors
register to vote
Was his great-great grandfather
who sharecropped for over 30 years
but somehow never could repay
even half the debt for the land promised him
And his father before him
who hung from a tree
for some reason no court record
ever could explain

No more than I can explain
to this six-year-old child
why his daddy seems so angry at times
Yes, his blood boils,
even in my veins
and I will not stand humbly by
allowing his denigration
through commission of silent complicity
for he is my brother
and I will honor his struggle
for dignity and life
with my own.

VICTORY SONG

Many have tried to deny me this
Tried to convince me this is not my due
Tried to convince me that I have not
earned this
That I could not handle this
That I should not expect this

But this victory is mine
I claim it now
I will not be denied this
Because I, and too many others
Have suffered too long and too hard
Laying the groundwork
Preparing for the victory of this day

I will not be denied this because
Too many have sacrificed too much
With the expectation that
Even though the victory would not be theirs
This day would come
Too many have taken pride
In contributing to this victory
The price has been paid
With the blood of my sisters and brothers
Foremothers and forefathers
This victory will be paid for
Even with the blood of tomorrow's children
Who will have no victory song of their own

Yes, this victory is mine
It is my birthright

I can handle this
I know what is required of me
What has been given up for me
I am willing to assume the responsibility
That awaits me in claiming this victory
And if you are about the business
Of making tomorrow better than yesterday
Then this victory also belongs to you

Reality Has No Rehearsals

REGRETS

Phantom echoes
Of missed opportunity
haunt us forever
in the eternity
called tomorrow

THE RACE

I raced along the edge of a cloud today
Trying desperately to beat the rain
How very symbolic, I mused
As in my mind's eye
Emerged an image of a woman
Frantically trying to outpace life
How ironic that a summer's rain
Should not be welcomed
Does not the rain replenish
Is it not through the rain that life is sustained
I stopped running
And was overtaken by the rain
The warm, embracing, invigorating rain
I laughed aloud as I welcomed my new friend

WHY NOT

I knew I'd never do it
I couldn't
I always wanted to
But didn't know how
Didn't even know where to start

All my life I'd been told
You can't do that
So I never questioned why
Just accepted that I couldn't
Til one day I asked myself, "Why not?"

Nothing beats a failure but a try
How often I've heard those words
Is that all they are – empty words
Or could they hold the key
OK, so I can't do it now
Does that mean I can never do it
What part can't I do
What part can I do
Will my ego stop me from trying
Because I fear I might fail
If I get over this fear
How far can I go

Until now I never believed I could do this
Never believed in myself enough to try
What else might I try if I succeed
What other fears might I conquer
Even if I fail
Will things be worse than before

Maybe that's the key –
That by challenging myself
I can discover new facets of me
Maybe by venturing beyond the safe and charted route
By striving toward goals once believed unattainable
I can achieve successes I never dreamed possible
Successes that I could never have known
Without having tried or having asked "Why not?"

MEMORIES

(Dedicated to those who lost loved ones in Oklahoma in April, 1996)

A building crumbled
As lives were stolen
By thieves who knew not their victims
The Blast left us each with our own pain
Full of emptiness
As we search for answers
Of why *our* loved ones
Why *this* time and place
We hold dear to our memories
Validated by photographs and mementos
Trinkets once thought trivial
Holding images of a yesterday
Unveiled by fate
As our special time of together
I carry these trinkets in my heart
And will remember you
And yesterday
Forever

MY MOTHER'S SMILE

Saw your smile in my mirror today
As always, it was good to see you
Yesterday, in remembrance of
My favorite childhood garden game
I picked Buttercups from our back yard
And sprinkled them over your grave
Yes, I still like butter
Thirty years have not dried the tears
Of an eight-year-old girl
Missing her mother's tender smile
and warm embrace
So I'll embrace your smile
Each time my mirror
Captures that special glow
Letting me know
Every once in a while
That you are with me
Still

VISITATION RITES

Like a pit to the flesh
Of an unripened peach
The girl-child clung to the hand
That held so many warm memories
Of distant yesterdays
The hand that worked so delicately
To wipe away the tears of too many good-byes
This visit like each before would be brief
For others did not welcome
Such warm hands
The girl-child, innocently defiant,
Rejoiced in the sunshine of the moment
All the while knowing
That the delicate work
Of the warm hand
Would soon begin

YOU, LIKE ME

(for Brenda)

You, like me
Are moved by the little things

You, like me
Weep silently through your pain

You, like me
Are strong, but grow weary from the struggle

You, like me
Need to understand and be understood

You, like me
Will flourish, despite fate's cruel hand

For you are my sister
And you, like me, are loved

I BE DANCIN'

Head swayin'
Body twistin'
Movin' like I got no bones
Music reachin' deep inside
Way down to my soul
I be dancin'

Hips rockin'
Feet stompin'
Poundin' to the beat
Eyes flashin'
Lips poutin'
I don't even want no seat
I be dancin'

Back archin'
Hands reachin'
Drum beat pulsin' through my veins
Chest heavin'
Breathin' hard
Congo beat take me away
I be dancin'

Legs struttin'
Feet on fire
Movin' to put out the flames
Guys be tryin' to run their games
I don't have time to play
I be dancin'

Can't they see?

I be steppin’
I be movin’
I be dancin’

THEY DON'T PLAY
(for Donna Curtis and Vince Evans)

She doesn't play the bass
Any more than he plays the piano
Their syncopated rhythms and relaxing vibrations
Feed your spirit
Like church feeds your soul
You can't call this play

Valentines aren't meant to be funny
And Georgia becomes a state of ecstasy
As the balladeer sings and the graceful strings
Of her bass transport you to a place
So sweet and serene
The world is a universe away
No, this is definitely not play

Serving up sassy rhythms
More seductive than a master masseuse
She thumps, strokes and bows her bass
Which, locked in her embrace,
Yields to strength and grace
Releasing a pitch richer than a mere
human ear can hear
No, nobody's playing here.

A duet of magical hands prance
On keys and strings as the vocalist sings
Jazz classics through the night
You watch their fanciful flight, but try
as you might
Your eyes loose sight of their steps…
Relax, catch your breath

Better yet, catch the A Train to Ellington's on
Thursdays, cause
Nobody's playing there.

THIS THING I DO

This thing I do with verse
Is like the surgeon severing synapses
To relieve schizophrenic episodes

It is here on dead trees
I do battle with demons
Whose vice-like grip
Constrict utterance of either
Prayer or condemnation

I deftly dance the tightrope
Between insanity and death
Uncertain at times which would bring
greater relief

But for my pen, this mystery
Would have long been revealed
And this thing I do with verse
Would be undone

POETRY MAN

From the moment I heard
Him utter his first verse
This master of metaphor
And his craft honed so fine
Performed dazzling duets
Both surreal and sublime
I did cerebral somersaults
Just to stay on top of his rhyme

This gold-medalled lyricist
Whose command of meter and style
Were so flawlessly fused
He whirled victims with lesser skills aside

I performed every manner
Of mental calisthenics,
Contortions which caressed each crevice
of my right hemisphere
Still he blew my mind

In this place where he reigns supreme
I sit entranced
As luscious gems, verses sweeter
Than any passion-fruit nectar
Drip like honey from his ebony lips
I scavenge every drop

His words intoxicate me beyond reason
His rhythm catapults my soul
To height of euphoria never before unleashed
Although fate has mastered this chance

encounter –
A shared moment of space and time
I dare not linger
For ours would be the cataclysm of two worlds
Destined to pursue divergent paths
Aware, yet undeterred
I anxiously anticipate the next collision.

THE REAL DEAL

It's real hard for me
To deal with me
Maneuvering over, under and around
My pains and disappointments
You thought I had it all together
'Cause I do my stuff so good
I keep myself so busy
Nobody ever stops to notice
I can't possibly have time
To take care of me

I raise my kids
Feed and love my man
Go to night school
Work eight hours plus everyday
On my good government job
Who in their right mind would think
Something was wrong

But sometime
I'm just fillin' time,
Just passin' time
Sometime, I'm just killin' time
Sometime though, time comes knockin'
on my front door
And stares me square in my face
Waitin' on me to do my stuff
And I can't do that fillin,' and passin' and
killin' stuff no more
Cause over time I've learned
That time's got a real deal of his own

SNAPSHOTS OF TRAIN #29

Disengaged smoldering cars
Strewn zigzag across once parallel
Strips of metallic ribbon

Mangled double-diesel engines
Belching fiery billows of black smoke
Against a backdrop of freshly fallen snow

Shrill sirens screaming
Toward havens of safety
While despondent loved-ones
Unappeased by explanations of "switch
problems"
Pray beside bloodstained gurneys

The grisly carnage
Of twisted locomotives
And eleven derailed lives
Headed, but not destined, for Chicago

GIVING THANKS

You don't remember me anymore
but for eight years, I was your daughter.
You and your beautiful wife opened your hearts
and home to my sisters and me
as you had to several other children over the
years.
But today, as you celebrate your birthday,
only slightly remembering Lillie, to whom you
were married for almost fifty years,
you don't remember who I am.
I think selfishly back to a yesteryear
when you made me heir to your family's legacy;
a sense of pride, a quest for knowledge,
and the self-esteem that only strong family ties
can forge.
But today, you don't remember who I am.
Now, when I look at you, it rocks the very
foundation that you and Mama Lillie gave me;
the one upon which I continue to build my
fortress,
safeguarding against the woulda' beens and
coulda' beens of yesterday and tomorrow.
When I see you I get frightened
for, if all that you were and had can be gone
then what of all that I desperately cling to today?
I still remember what you have long since
forgot;
that you were a Tuskeegee, Howard and
American University
graduate who earned a Ph.D. in Theology,
And that your personal library of classic novels

and resource books
were the playground and movie house of
my youth,
that you pastored for over fifty years
preaching sermons that cloaked me in spiritual
armor long before I understood the storms
against which I would do battle,
that you hosted a morning radio talk show
addressing social and spiritual issues
that frame the messages I lift in my
poetry today,
that not only were you there when Dr. King
delivered his "I Have A Dream" speech,
but you had been, and continued to live the
dream long before and long after he spoke those
now famous words,
that you were a man of God, an intellectual,
a stern disciplinarian and a good father
who still had the humility to sweep the kitchen
floor when it was needed
—although you usually wore your hat while
doing so.
You were not one to give hugs or kisses,
but we knew you cared by your presence and
your deeds,
and now, you don't even remember me,
and it hurts that I can't say "Thank You"
in a way that you can understand
all that I need to say "Thank You" for,
but I'll say it anyway.
Thank you Rev. Craig, for being Daddy
And oh, by the way,
Happy 95th Birthday.

750 HORSES (Virgin Ride)

My senses flood
At the onslaught of panoramic scenes
Motionless, yet in perpetual motion
Visions of summer’s regal splendor
Rapidly unfold before me
Then vanish
In an intoxicating instant
As if they, themselves sense my inability
To withstand such intense pleasure prolonged

I desperately attempt to commit to memory
The magnificence of the moment
All the while keenly aware
That only my borrowed helmet
Protects me from
The thunderous roar and peril
Of each eighteen-wheeled semi we pass

The highway beckons the driver
And his captivated passenger
To throw caution to the wind
The occasional spasmodic thrust
Of 750 horses
Jolts me back to reality
I tighten my hold
And ride

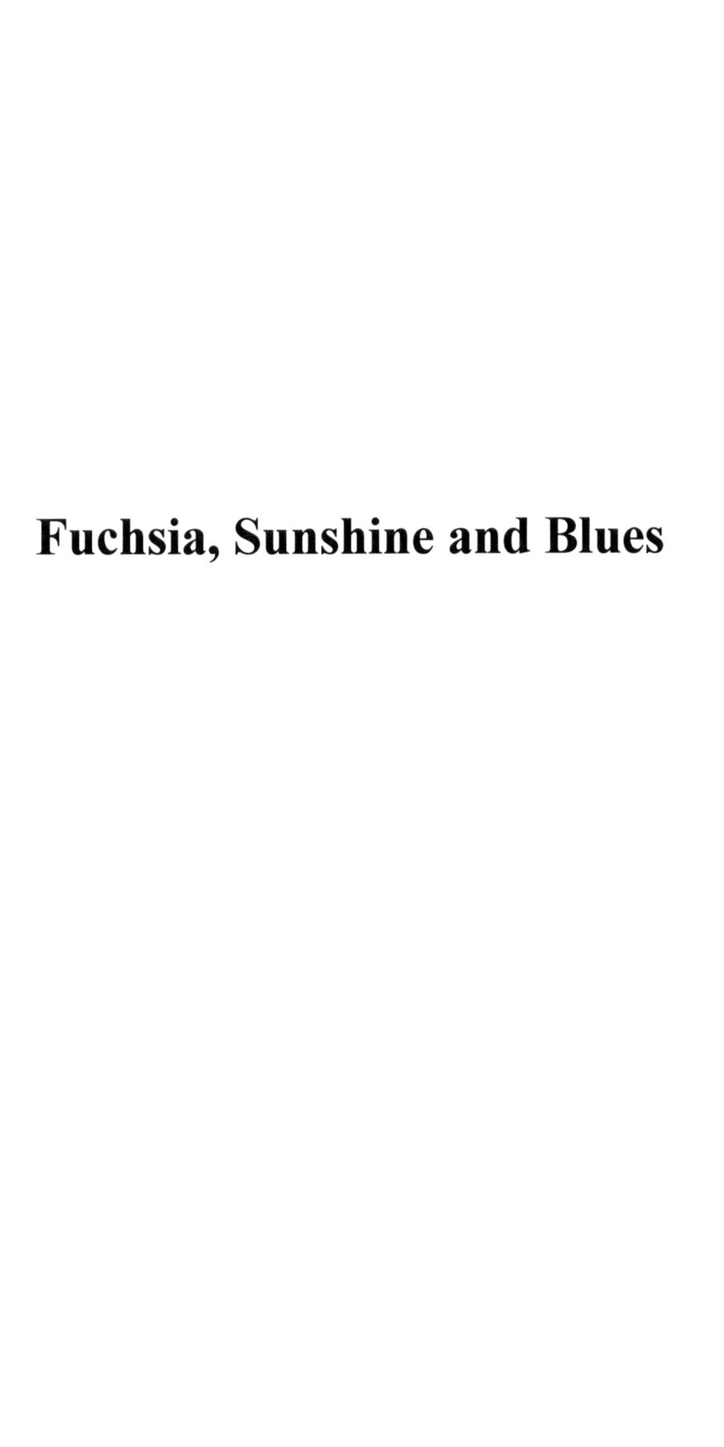

Fuchsia, Sunshine and Blues

COMING INTO FOCUS

As I wipe the steam from my mirror
In the morning of my years
The blurred vision of youth
Captures a luminescent illusion of perfection

As I wipe the steam from my mirror
Truth, previously concealed
Reveals a time-tarnished image
Blemished by broken dreams
And promises of passions yet fulfilled

As I wipe the steam from my mirror
I erase the slate of yesterday's
disappointments
Undaunted, my vision of tomorrow
Glistens with crystal clarity

As I wipe the steam from my mirror
I marvel at the magnificence of persistence
And smile as a picture perfect reality
Finally comes into focus

LOWER LEFT SIDE

I listened to his eloquent articulation for hours
Followed from floor to floor as he unraveled
the mysteries and
explained the intricacies of vernacular art
Later sat gazing intently upon the wood
burning stove
as I feigned disregard for the splendor of the
truest masterpiece
residing in this galleried abode
Of course I was impressed
Entranced even
But after the tour -
After the lesson on gifted souls
Whose self-devised language was more real
and raw than most could discern
I could only dream in tightly guarded reverie
of how the luscious lips of this gentle giant
whose grand stature was dwarfed only by his
integrity would feel pressed against
The lower left side
Of the small of my back.

ALL I EVER WANTED

All I ever wanted
Was someone to love me
Someone I respected
And who respected me in return
Someone who cared what I thought about
And wanted out of life
Didn't necessarily have to share all my views
But at least acknowledged my choices
And my right to them
So how did I turn out to be
The one who did him wrong
I'd told him up front about me, my choices,
my limitations,
I told him mine and he told me his
So I thought
I told him I couldn't give what I didn't have
Told him not to expect what I couldn't give
Cause I been givin' all my life
Givin' and makin' too many choices
based on fear
Fearin' almost everything I couldn't control
Knowing I couldn't control much of anything
And was tired of trying to control everything
But lately, mostly feared being out of control
So the last thing a woman
Divorced after 25 plus years of marriage
3 children, 30 years of 9 to 5,
and a burning desire to feel –
finally feel the passions that she somehow
miraculously finds herself still capable
of feeling
the last thing that woman wants to hear is

somebody – anybody
Sayin' "You got to get beyond
Lookin' at the world though rose-colored
glasses with your name on 'em"
Or somebody tellin' her she's got to accept
that what other folks think about her matters
so much it ends up makin' choices for her.
No, I just don't have no more of that to give
Not to a man, a child, a job
Not to nothin'
But he wouldn't hear me
Talked 'bout me being selfish and rigid
Talked about things
So wrapped in and warped by my past
Wasn't no way a future could be built
Even had me trippin' for a minute, believin' I
could — We could
And on top of everything else
Expected me to be like
Other women and act like I cared what
Somebody else thought
About my life – if they weren't in it
My image – if they didn't approve
About the people I love when fate
smiles on me
Enough to let me
But this man
This educated, respectable, principled man
This homespun, character-driven man
This unexpectedly erotic, would love to be
sensitive, oh so patient man
That I love as much as I admire
And whose love I fear twice as much as both

And curse the day I ever let myself do either
Gets under my skin and on my last nerve
And he just don't, won't understand
That the best gift I ever gave him
Was his freedom.

MOURNING

Sometimes when I first wake up
I forget my bed is half empty
That only my shoes fill my closet
That no strong hands still stroke my thighs

Sometimes when I first wake up
I forget only my breakfast needs fixing
That no one steams my mirror while shaving
Or leaves my toilet seat up

I forget that brewing coffee for one
takes only two scoops
That single egg omelets just don't work
And reading the sports page aloud - - alone
makes no sense
Sometimes I forget

I wake up remembering
your scent on my pillow
Your hands caressing me gently
Your soft lips kissing my neck
Then my heart remembers
the stabbing dagger of betrayal
the day I saw you with her
Like high tide crashing against jagged shores
Reality comes flooding back
And I wipe away yet another tear
That seeped out of the reservoir of yesterday's
flood
Damned by a woman
Determined not to drown.

PLEASE

If this is what it takes
Let me sustain this rage
Let me not forget this pain
Let me be strong in my lonely hours
Let me get you out of my mind
Get you out of my life
Let me grow to know you are not for me
Let me go
Please

THE GULL

Like driftwood
I submerge and resurface
Amidst life's turbulent currents
A lone weary gull seeking shelter
Chanced to rest amongst my broken boughs
His touch was so gentle, so light
Yet his hold firm and sure
Evoking unexpected waves within me
Mightier than the greatest crest during any storm
For a moment I forgot my nautical struggle
Only to submerge more deeply than ever
Into an abyss of loneliness
For as with all sea gulls
Who are no longer in need of shelter
Who alight only to rest
Having done so
He promptly
Left

CONSUMED

Standing tall, majestically poised
She awaited the moment
He would set her on fire
Consuming the very essence
Of her being
She would have it no other way
For without him she was useless
Mere adornment –
Beautiful, but hard and cold
All her life she had been
Placed upon a pedestal
For distant eyes to gaze upon
Her outward beauty
Yet she yearned to be consumed
Yearned to give true meaning to her existence
Her body
Ignited by his slightest touch
Now melted
As he sank deeper inside her
Her fragrance permeated the room
As she wept hot waxen tears
Like each of her sisters before
She too would soon dissipate
Into nothingness
The radiance and warmth
That were hers just a few
Short hours before
Linger as faded memories
Where once this elegant
Queen stood tall

Only smoldering embers remain
Their union
Pre-ordained by fate
The perfect match
Consumed them both
This virgin-no-more
Could never know
The pleasures of the flesh
For she was but a candle
Consumed by her persistent lover
The flame

THE SCENT

It washed over her
Consuming her like the night
Passion burning throughout every fiber
The scent of his love
She was powerless against it

Wet with anticipation
She trembled as she approached
The place that only he could take her
The scent of his love
She craved it ravenously

She gulped the crisp night air
Her nostrils flaring wildly
As she took in all that she could
The scent of his love
She languished in the rapture of it

Inside this realm of ecstasy
Released, their souls became one
Eternity's instant, too brief this moment to contain
The scent of their love – lingered
She prayed never to be free of it

MY FINE CHOCOLATE BROTHER

I want you
my fine chocolate brother
all over me
Want you all up inside
my mind and soul
every part of me
Want you inside my mind
so you can know what I'm about.
Want you inside my soul
so that our strength can forge as one.
But I don't just want you inside my mind and soul.
On no, my fine chocolate Brother,
I want you pourin' over me
like caramel over a golden apple.
Want to feel your impulses flood my ocean;
Want to swim to and sleep on the shores of your smile.
You see, I'm proud to be the one
who makes real your fantasies
and I intend to give you more
than you even conceived in your dreams
Because I get a thrill,
and no, I could never get my fill of you,
my fine chocolate brother.

POINT OF NO RETURN

Like a cookie jar to a small child on tiptoe
You keep your emotions just out of reach
Like the on-again, off-again flickering of a
half-screwed bulb
Your ambivalent come-ons too often leave me
in the dark
Like a passion fruit pop-sickle left on a
summer sidewalk
You leave me soaked with my favorite
fragrance
But unable to taste it
Like Mario Andretti running out of gas
Ten feet before the finish line
The absurdity of your exits has taken me
Past the point-of-no-return
Just know that the last time
Was the last time
You'll ever cross my finish line

PORK CHOPS AND TWINKIES

The avowed vegetarian of seventeen years
Gnawed pork chops and Twinkies while
fighting back tears
"Wedding Bliss" read the caption in the Jet
magazine
Depicting her lover and some other Nubian
queen
Tossing the third bone on top of the heap
Nightmares soon denied her the solace of
sleep
Revenge, her new ally, called for serious
measures
Against this lech who'd embezzled her most
precious of treasures
After pulling one last Twinkie from the now
empty box
She changed phone numbers, alarm codes, car
and door locks
Now donning an admittedly sinister grin
She sought postal regulations from a very
discreet friend
Delivery of animals, she learned, is
permitted by law
Although tightly controlled, offered the
opportunity she sought
She wrapped the wedding gift with extreme
trepidation
Air holes camouflaged by nuptial decoration
She felt it befitting, the perfect irony
Her one true regret, that she would not be
there to see

But the prospect nonetheless pleased her immeasurably
The thought of one six foot snake
Bestowing the gift of freedom upon another

Tomorrow's Promise

ODE TO MY TEN-YEAR-OLD CHILD

(for Rashaad)

Oh child o' mine,
what's it gon' take
to get you outta bed
so we won't be late.
Ev'ry mornin' when I try to get you up
you don't move one inch 'til I whip your butt.
Why won't you just do
what you know you 'sposed to?
Instead, every mornin' you just
lay there 'til I start to fuss.
You're not the only one who gets hurt
'cause when you're late for school, I'm late
for work.
The world don't stop spinning 'cause you
wanna sleep
and if I loose my job, we'll be out on the street
Won't you please get up, let's get movin'
cause this is one battle that we're both loosin'.
Let's start our days with breakfast and hugs
instead of this war, let's start off with love.
Come one, hurry up, please get dressed.
Let's both agree to give it our best.
I know you can do this,
and I'll help you get through this.
So today I pray
I can put my belt away,
'cause I love you child o' mine
and I'm sho' tired o' fussin
and whippin' your behind.

BEAUTY PARLOR MESS

When I was a child
Mama said, "Girl, don't you know you been blessed?"
Said she didn't know where I come from
with all that beauty parlor mess
Besides, you're too young to get your hair pressed
Get on up in this chair
so I can braid your hair
Hand me that jar of Vaseline
Mama was just plain mean!

Couldn't wait 'til I was grown
Made me an appointment on my own
Sat in that beauty parlor chair
Told that lady to perm, cut and color my hair!
Couldn't tell me nothin'
Knew I was lookin' good
My hair looked smooth and shiny
just like I knew that it would.

It's been quite a few years
since my first day in that chair
That first time was fun
then for years, I had to go there.
Nobody told me about lye
and how perm changes your hair.
Nobody told me about the costs
Now these are secrets that women should - but don't share.

My daughter recently reminded me
that she's now in the sixth grade.
Told me she was too old
to still be wearing braids.
I look at her long, thick lovely black hair
and think back to my first beauty parlor chair.
Then I say, "Girl, don't you know you been
blessed?"
Forget about all that beauty parlor mess!

JUST AROUND THE CORNER

It's just around the corner
He'd heard grandma say
But for all his searching
His three-year-old eyes
Could find no such thing
As the magical, elusive spring
He peered around each corner he encountered
In search of rabbits, flowers and green things
But found no sign of the thing called spring
He hid amongst the barren branches
Of the forsythia bush
Spying on his back yard
Which corner, he'd plead
As Grandma wiped red mud
From pudgy hands and soiled knees of
corduroy pants
When will spring stop hiding?
Her soft hug and warm Grandma laugh
reassured
The anticipating eyes now clouding with
doubt
That spring was near and would soon appear
"Soon chile," said Grandma, "real soon."

TO SEE A TREE SNEEZE

(for Kayla, Aaliyah and Joy)

Wouldn't it be great to see
A snow covered tree sneeze
Or hiccup?
I'd lay underneath with my arms open wide
As she shed her winter coat down onto me.
Then to thank God for sharing
His beauty with the world
I'd make snow angels
To send the snow
Back to heaven again

TEN THOUSAND ANGELS DANCING

(for Joy Danielle)

A celestial rainbow adorned the sky
The day God gifted me with you
He blessed you with a heart
As radiant as your smile
He gave you the wisdom of Solomon
The speed of a gazelle
And the power and grace
Of ten thousand angels
Dancing in your soul
Feel the rhythm of their dance
In the beating of your heart
Their song resounds throughout the universe
Listen well, their melodies foretell
Tomorrow's promise
Unfulfilled, they become eternity's regrets
With a whisper, the least of them
Defeats your mightiest foe
The swiftest carries you
With lightening speed through life's hurdles
And shields you from harm
The most compassionate stands ready
To mend a broken heart
For with a heart so large
Breaks are sure to come
Let their trumpets guide you nightly
To playful dreams
Where you dance with your heavenly guardians
Then awaken refreshed and renewed in God's love

I am so proud He chose to give you life
through me
He too is proud
For you share His light for others to see
It is through you
And thousands more with your spirit
That tomorrow offers the world a new day
And even after the tomorrows
When I dance with your angels
Know that God's love and mine
Will continue to shine
Through you

BRIAN'S FAVORITE BREAKFAST

I climb up on the counter
And get the box down from the shelf
Mom measures the exact amount
Then lets me mix it by myself
She heats up the skillet
Saying, "Stay back now, this is hot!"
My sister and I are hungry
So we ask mom to fix a lot
PSSSSSSSSSSSSSSSSSSST!
What a wonderful sound they make
I rush to get the butter
Neither of us can hardly wait
Mom gives me the first one
My sister gets the next three
Dad slowly pours the syrup
Then he cuts mine up for me
MMMMMMMMMMMMMM!
The whole house smells great
Nothing ever tastes as good
As a stack of mom's pancakes!

DANIELLE'S PICTURE

My daughter drew a picture of herself at school
Brought it home and gave it to me
Oh, what a wonderful funny face
I shall treasure it eternally

She drew a smile so broad, so wide
Tied her hair with a ribbon of red
She made her eyes shine brightly
Then placed a beaming sun over her head

The smile tells me she is happy
As she basks proudly in the sun's rays
The size of her portrait is significant
Her face covers half the page

Twenty-four meticulously drawn eye-lashes
On a face so beautiful and brown
Boasting no feature too trivial to portray
Ears protruding – one up, one slightly down

My daughter drew her picture at school today
I am so very glad to see
The happiness and joy it shows
This means a lot to me

I look at my daughter's self-portrait
As a symbolic piece of artistry
Because children often say more
through pictures
Than they ever express verbally

Yes, I'm proud of my daughter's precious gift
And all that it portrays
But her face aglow as she presented it
Is the picture I will cherish always.

BLESSINGS OF SISTER-LOVE

(for my twin nieces, Kayla and Aaliyah)

Thank you Father for my sister
And thank you for Your Holy Spirit
In me and in her
May we forever be together
And forever be with You
So that we may never be alone
Thank you for giving me my sister
To grow up with, to play with,
To learn with, and share with
Each and every day
Thank you for my sister
To watch over me and whom I will watch over
Even as You watch over us
Each and every day
If I have food,
Let me share it with her
If I have shelter,
Let me always protect her from
danger or harm
But let us remember always Father
That You are our greatest protector
Let us know that Your love will feed us when
we are hungry
And quench us when we are thirsty
Let us know that the light from Your goodness
Is our guide when we are lost
And that the power of Your greatness
Is our strength when we are afraid
For You God are good and great
We love and honor you God

But we know that You love us
More than we love ourselves
We thank you God for the blessings
of sister-love
In the precious name of Your Son
Jesus Christ, Amen.

Brevity, Beauty and *Basho
(Haiku)

*Matsuo Basho (1644-1694), a Zen Buddhist who was an accomplished haiku poet. Haiku, a genre of poetry with its origins in Japan, is widely known for its brevity. Each poem consists of 17 syllables."

HAIKU #33 - (Midnight Melodies)

Cricket whispers pierce
nocturnal silence. Their songs
Awaken the dawn

HAIKU #315 - (Morning Song)

The crow's mating call
cuts through the crisp morning air
waking me from sleep

HAIKU #316 – (Spring Morn)

Budding branches sway
Butterflies light on petals
kissed by April's tears

HAIKU #513 - (Sweet Sounds)

Whispers in my ear
sound so sweet, just like honey
dripping down my thighs

HAIKU #317 - (Mountain View)

Swallows warm their wings
feed and dance in mountain air
Oh Shenandoah!

HAIKU # 318 - (Winter's Warning)

Bare winter branches
paint a cold October sky
their breeze bids birds "fly!"

HAIKU #3 - (Digital Clock)

Like 12:59
lovers' lies say it's time
to start over again

HAIKU #325 - (School Zones)

Bright yellow convoys
controlling more than traffic
transport precious cargo

Reachin' Up

GET OUTTA MY WAY

Would somebody please tell yesterday
To get outta' my way
Tell her to stop bulldozin' my dreams
Stop tramplin' my tomorrows
And knockin' me down ever' time I try to get ahead

Would somebody please tell yesterday
To git on back to where hope be broke
An' choice be gone, so me and mine
Can stand a chance to rise above yesterday's can'ts

Now I know yesterday been around
a long time
She prob'ly figure she gon' be here fo'ever
She done seen the new millennium come in
Lotta' folks didn't you know
'Cause o' yesterday
Lotta' young folk – yesterday took 'em
'Course she took a lotta' old folks too
Took my mama an' daddy

Yesterday jes' keep on takin' an' takin'
Takin' folks an' they dreams an' they hopes
She take anything ain't locked down I s'pose
That's why I be real careful these days
'Cause I'm tired o' yesterday showin' up all over the place

You see I been workin' too hard

Tryin' to keep my stuff together
Gittin' ready fo' tomorrow
Fo' yesterday to 'jes come up in here
And take it all away
But when a body don't lock they stuff up tight
Doin' what's right
Stayin' two steps ahead o' yesterday
Wid a stick in one hand
And a Bible in the other
Yesterday can sho' 'nuf knock you down
Keep yo' dreams from eva' gettin' off the
ground

Well I say, yesterday done took enough
So I put locks on all my stuff
My soul be locked on Jesus
My heart be locked on my man
My children be locked in the cradle of my
love
Wid my two strong hands guidin' 'em
Showin' 'em the way – away from yesterday
My home be locked in a sacred shield
Anointed wid God's special blessin's
Cause ain't nobody messin' wid somethin' I
worked that hard fo'
My job be locked down wid twenty-plus years
o' hard work
Wid me prayin' that I be movin' in the right
direction

Yeah, I got locks on all my stuff
And I be ready fo' tomorrow
So somebody please tell yesterday

To stay outta' my way
'Cause it's time fo' tomorrow to let her
light shine
And one thing's fo' sho'
Tomorrow's the one place yesterday can't go

WALK WITH ME LORD

(In grateful appreciation, to Vince)

Walk with me Lord,
Walk through my mind
And teach me to follow your lead
And heed your word and way

Walk inside my soul Lord
Walk inside my soul and just have your way
Fill me with grace and humility
Let me overflow with Your spirit of Love
Fill me so full all I can do is Your will, Lord
Walk with me.

Walk with me Lord,
Walk with me to the place of understanding
How I'm s'pose to do what "thus saith the Lord"
Walk with me so I feel you holdin' my hand
Keepin' me strong when I'm in my valleys, Lord
And walk with me to lift me to the high places, Lord
But not so high that I look down
On my sisters and brothers who's strugglin' to find their way,
Or don't even know that they are lost
Walk with me Lord

Walk with me out on the street Lord
To touch your children out on the street
And give them sight to light their way

But not just sight for them Lord,
Give sight to their neighbors whose eyes are blind
To sorrow and crime until in touches them
Walk with me Lord

Walk with me Lord, into the schoolhouses
To touch the teachers to whom we've entrusted our children –
Your most precious gift.
Build a hedge of protection
Around the schools and the teachers and the children, Lord
So they may be shielded from on high
Shine Your light as you walk with them Lord
Teaching them that the brightest tomorrow
Comes with a strong mind and an humble spirit
Teach them how they too can be made all-powerful
By knowledge of Your word
Walk with me Lord

Walk with us in this place Lord
Bless your children gathered here
But bless also your children who are far from home
Let them know they are never far from our hearts
Bless them and protect them wherever they go
Let them hear the songs of praise
Lifted by your servants in this place
And feel Your mighty power

Let us all walk with you Lord
So that we, ourselves, may be lifted
As we lift up praise to your Holy name

CHALICES
(for John)

If God put His son through The Cross,
How little of us is asked when
We are given life's challenges.
Challenges that appear to be
The burdens of the world on our shoulders.
They are, in fact, but a speck of sand
On the shores of the universe.
The most tumultuous ordeal
But the shift of a single hair on God's head.
Every challenge - He predestined
At the dawn of time when He set creation
into motion.
He has already wept for our pain
And His tears created the oceans and the seas.
He has reveled in our victories
And His joy burst forth as the beaming sun.
When mountains and valleys seem to
delay our journey,
And detour us from our destination,
God wants us to remember that our true destination
Is at His side in Glory.
What we may view as mountains and valleys
Are, in reality, signposts illuminating our paths.
We must understand that life's challenges
are put there,
Not to overwhelm or break us,
But rather, they are merely God's fingers
Gently shaping and molding us
From empty vessels of clay
Into overflowing chalices of pure gold.

WE WANDER

We wander through life's pastures
Grazing indiscriminately on all before us
Expecting somehow only the wheat, not the chaff
To nourish us
For sustenance from chaff is foul
And causes our bellies anguish
Much as sustenance from sin
Causes anguish to our soul, and to God
We seek to soothe our torment
With promises of discernment
Expecting God to bargain in our terms
But we fail to acknowledge
That our pain is His pain
And He wants more for us
Than we, in our greediest and most selfish hour
Could possibly conceive
He merely asks that we lift our eyes
From their downcast glance
And follow His light
Acknowledging from whence cometh the light,
And the wheat,
And even the chaff
For without Him
We would forever be
Lost sheep

NO CONSTRAINTS

My Mind
Unaware of the constraints some would
impose
Forever seeks knowledge from the tree of life

My body
Unaware of the constraints some would
impose
Glistens proud and strong in the sun's rays
Which have bronzed it beautiful

My soul
Unaware of the constraints some would
impose
Conquers demons and lifts prayers of
jubilation to my God

His Spirit
Showers my mind, body and soul
Empowering me to excel as though I were
Unaware of the constraints some would
impose

SISTER TO SISTER

(Dedicated in power and praise to my sisters in Collective Voices)

Sharing spirit-filled blessings, we soar
With faith as the source of our power
It is real
For through God we receive all
God and His glory are awesome
His power so great
The tiny blade of grass withstands
The trampling stampedes of mighty beasts
The dove's delicate feather
Defeats the raging storm
Delivering it safely home
And the Collective Voices of sisters
Who lift His word shall be heard around the world
Be still my sisters
And rejoice in His gift
For the dawn of tomorrow
Glows on the precipice
And there is much work to be done

BASICS

I am a woman of basics.
Basic meals
I like meat and potatoes.
Dessert if I want.
No diet.
Drive a Honda
See what I mean?
Basic.
Nothing special in my appeal.
Just basically seeking to be in touch
To connect with His Spirit.
My work is basic
Lift up the Word
Basic.
Share the power
Basic.
Seek out paths
That guide me to that place
Of insight and peace.
I need to deal in basics.
Yes, no, black, white
Red works just fine.
Never did like gray,
Pink and yellow give me problems
Cause conflict in my soul.
When I have a question
I ask it.
When I ask a question
I want an answer,
Basic
Direct

Complete,
Like my need to be.

WHISTLING WINDS

(to Susan at Bishop Clagette Center)

Morning winds whistling
Through pains of unfitted glass
Awaken my soul
As Sonbeams light the east bedroom
Of this Old Farmhouse
They clear away the clutter
And illuminate my path
Reflections of yesterday
Laden with dormant messages
That have been waiting
For this place, 'til this time
Ready me for tomorrow
The songs of the whistling winds
In this place of solitude
Tell me to go forward
With uplifted eyes
They will forever remind me
When the clutter returns
When I am detoured off my path
To go forward
With uplifted eyes

HUNGER

To hunger
To be so in need of sustenance
That the lessening of pain
Becomes one's entire life focus
Societal mores become unaffordable luxuries
Faint from fear and need
We become driven by nature's primal force
To survive

I have known such hunger
I have felt such pain
My God reached out to me
In the midst of my devastation
His was the only sustenance
That satisfied my hunger
His was the only force
Greater than pain
His was the power of love